D1527855

A

Craftsman at Play

in

Creation

Poems

by

Jake Frost

For Gloria

Table of Contents

Poems for Christmas

The Craftsman

. . . recognize the Craftsman while paying heed to His works . . .

Wisdom 13, 1

. . . fire or wind or swift air, or the circle of the stars, or turbulent water, or the luminaries of heaven . . . through delight in the beauty of these things . . . know how much better than these is their Lord, for the Author of Beauty created them. And if men were amazed at their power and working, let them perceive from them how much more powerful is He Who formed them. For from the greatness and beauty of created things comes a corresponding perception of their Creator.

Wisdom 13, 2-5

In the Beginning

In the beginning was the Word, and the Word was with God, and the Word was God. He was in the beginning with God; all things were made through Him, and without Him was not anything made that was made. In Him was life, and the life was the light of men.

John, 1, 1-4

In the beginning God created the heavens and the earth . . . And God saw everything that He had made, and behold, it was very good.

Genesis 1, 1 & 31

. . . He established the heavens . . . He drew a circle on the face of the deep . . . He made firm the skies above . . . He established the fountains of the deep . . . He assigned the sea its limit . . . He marked out the foundations of the earth . . .

Proverbs 8, 27-30

"Where were you when I laid the foundation of the earth? . . .determined its measurements . . . stretched the line upon it . . . [when] its bases [were] sunk . . . laid its cornerstone, when the morning stars sang together, and all the sons of God shouted for joy?"

Job, 38, 4-7

A Craftsman at Play in Creation

He was a Craftsman at play in Creation
All things to Him a delight
When He laid the world's foundation
And divided from day the night

And it was in His image that we were made
The image of Three-in-One
So also is ours the game He played
When He forged the molten sun

That our minds, too, should conceive
And our hands bring forth to be
That in creating we perceive
The joy of the Trinity

Chapel of the Coimbras, Braga, Portugal

The Sweeping of the Waves

The sweeping of the waves
On the surface of the sea
Crash into the shore
Sculpting endlessly

The sinewy strand of sand,
Golden against the blue,
The way that God's creation
Is sculpting me and you

Our Maker's Mark

Everything the craftsman makes
Bears its maker's mark
Burned in wood or carved in stone
Showing clear and stark

Just as does the child's life
Show the parents' role
And each of us our Maker's mark
Bear within our soul

His Praises Shall Be Sung!

He rode a colt that all might know
Over the palms there came to them
The King of Peace as was foretold
That day into Jerusalem

The multitudes began to praise
God for His greatness and rejoice
For all His mighty works and raise
Glad Hosanas with all their voice

But Pharisees said to the King,
"Rebuke these people who proclaim,"
"Your Kingship and Hosanas sing,"
"As though You came in God's own name."

"If they were silent," said the King,
Above the people's joyous shout,
"Still to Heaven would praises ring,"
"For the very stones would then cry out!"

"... have you seen the storehouses of the hail,
which I have reserved for the time of trouble, for
the day of battle and war?"

Job 38, 22-23

The Giants Who Stride the Storm

When the giants who stride the storm
Roll in the sky their thunder-stones
Through the valleys the clouds have formed
Until the rattle's in your bones

And pump their bellows till the winds
Of tempest thrash the trees about
And hurl the hail from their cellar bins
And cast the lightning as they shout

Remember these are creatures, too,
Of The Lamb from Galilee
That have their role in His retinue
And learn to pray on bended knee

Note on The Fig Leaves

In his book, *You Can Understand the Bible*,
Peter Kreeft poses the question: Why did Adam
and Eve sew fig leaves after The Fall? His answer:
they fell for the temptation to be like God, but after
eating the fruit of The Tree of the Knowledge of
Good and Evil, it was glaringly obvious—in the
reality of their own bodies, in their very flesh
itself—that they were not gods. Neither of them
could, as their own bodies clearly revealed, create
life on their own. Their own bodies told them that
Man cannot create life in and of himself, nor can
Man sustain life in existence, not even his own.
Only God can. And when confronted with that
truth, Adam and Eve did what men so often do: try
to hide the truth, first and foremost from
themselves. So they sewed fig leaves to cover those
parts of their bodies which so obviously spoke the
truth they wished to deny, then hid from Truth
Himself in The Garden.

The Leaves of the Fig Were Sewn

The Holy Spirit in the sky
Writes in a hand that's vast
A message unto you and I
In the cosmos wheeling past

When burning sunset fades to black
When night gives way to day
Know the power that all things lack:
That they shall not fade away

For no things can keep, by tooth or claw,
Existence of their own
It was to hide from this, the truth they saw,
The leaves of the fig were sewn

Whence Shall Come the Beast?

Look now to the East
   Where the storm winds rise
   Whence shall come the beast
To end your wicked lies

In the thunder hear
Wherein speaks the Voice
Warning there draws near
Justice for your choice:

"Now for far too long
Wrath I have forbore
Turn now from your wrong
For wrath I stay no more!"

"Now your eyes shall weep
Your pride shall broken be
And sorrows on you heap
Until you turn to Me."

"Your cities now shall burn
And you shall know My rod
Until at last you learn
Who is like to God?"

Your Mighty Wind

A summer morning when the wind
Tosses about the trees
And stirs the grasses so they bend
And ripple like the seas

How beautiful the grasses grow
How mighty is the wind
That makes the wide prairie flow
Like oceans rolling in

Dear Lord please let Your mighty Wind
Move me like Your seas
And like Your waving grasses when
They stir within Your breeze

Read the Signs

A roaring wind swept through the sky
And thrashed the trees about
And everywhere its moan and cry
Resounded like a shout

As dark the storm clouds overhead
Cast all the land in gloom
Thus, *read the signs*, our Savior said,
To flee the coming doom

By a Power Beyond Its Own

Racing on the roaring wind
High up where the air is thinned

A crow carried on the gale
Stretches out its wings to sail

Streaking on across the sky
Flung upon the storm to fly

Through the heavens, changing fast
As upon the tempest blast

Swift the storm comes rolling in
Bringing dark and cloud and wind

And borne upon its leading edge
Where keen there whets the driving wedge

Like a bolt shot from the bow
On the storm there flies the crow

With a speed before unknown
By a power beyond its own

Sunrise over the Earth seen from space,
photo from NASA

Moon Ever Gazing on the Dawn

When the moon appears wispy white
High in a sky of blue
Lingering on after night
Into a day that's new

And looks upon a world that's bright
And across the world it sees the sun
Even from the realm of night
Beyond the edge where day's begun

The shining edge where first there burns
The morning's molten spark
As on its course the world that turns
Revolves again from dark

The burning line of dawn upon the Earth as seen from space, photo from NASA

Into the brightness of the day
Beyond the shining line
Following ever on the way
Fixed by the Hand Divine

The world through day and night moves on
And never is either done
Moon ever gazing on the dawn
Of ever rising sun

While the sun peers ever into night
And shines upon the moon
That reflects again its blazing light
While in-between we swoon

The moon seen over the edge of the Earth from space

Two Eagles in the Sky I Saw

Two eagles in the sky I saw
   Sail on wing and wind
   Spiraling without a flaw
High where the ether thinned

Somewhere in the in-between
Where two realms entwine
Below, the Earth of blue and green
Beyond, the stars that shine

From where they soared could both they see?
As can men from mountains high
Or the humble bowed on bended knee
Who peer beyond the sky

We Live Within a World of Storm

To see the calm after the storm
With the sea in quietude
And gentle breezes soft and warm
In a peaceful, morning mood

You'd never guess what lurks within
The ocean's mighty breast
How in the deep, like hidden sin
That waits to be confessed

Tempests in the dark yet brood
O that mortal man might learn!
The calm is but an interlude
Until the storms return

For we live within a world of storm
Where shakes the spear of war
A world that day and night both form
And lie ever at your door

Crows Like Kites Upon the Breeze

Crows like kites upon the breeze
Floating high above the trees

On shifting winds where they weave
Like ships that ride the heaving seas

And though the winds must ever blow
And drive the rains and falling snow

Yet amid their moan and cry
Wings outstretched mount to the sky

Men Say Their Prayers and Sail

The billows bare upon their crest
The barque of rope and wood
Over secrets in the deep unguessed
No man knows nor should

By canvas sheet and wooden spar
And the blowing of the gale
And the turning wheel and shining star
Men say their prayers and sail

Note on Potiphar and Joseph

After Joseph was sold into slavery by his
brothers, he became a slave in the house of
Potiphar the Egyptian. All things prospered in
Joseph's hands and Potiphar promoted Joseph,
until Joseph rose to run all of Potiphar's house.
But Joseph was handsome, and Potiphar's wife
desired him. She tried to force her affections on
him and Joseph fled, but she held his cloak and it
came off as he ran. Potiphar's wife accused Joseph
of attempted rape, presenting Joseph's cloak as

proof. Potiphar cast Joseph into prison. But from prison, Joseph rose again, eventually to rule a far greater house: that of Pharoah, and all of Egypt. Sitting at the right hand of Pharoah, Joseph gathered and dispensed the grain that all of Egypt, and the nation's beyond, came begging Pharoah for in order to survive the time of drought and famine which Joseph had foreseen in Pharoah's dream. Genesis, chapters 37-50.

When Potiphar Met Joseph Again

When Joseph was the steward
Ruling all of Pharoah's lands
Then came to him, begging bread,
Potiphar, with trembling hands

How could it be the one that he
Sent in chains into the prison
To rule all of Egypt's empire vast
Seated at Pharaoh's side had risen?

Joseph saw him quake and said,
"Have no fear for our past of strife,"
"I suspect that God has punished you,"
"Already through your wife."

Who Paid the Prophets Not Their Due

The tempest tossed the trees about
The leaves of autumn flew
And crows on wing with a raucous shout
Were flung on the winds that blew

Set astir in a world that shakes
When blows the mighty wind
Where trees crack and earth quakes
When the rumblings first begin

Of forces deep and forces old
From before the world's first day
That still through eons have their hold
And now shall have their way

Feel the tremors beneath your feet!
Feel the wind upon your face!
Unroll the scroll and read the sheet
Wherein the prophets trace

What things have been and yet will be
And ready your place to stand
For there's warning in the roaring sea
Of what comes unto this land

For in a moment all will change
And all things be overthrown
Leaving us a world turned strange
By hidden things made known

For though these things were always thus
To us they now seem new
For these things remained unknown to us
Who paid the prophets not their due

In the Dimness of the Morning Light

In the dim before the dawn's light,
That sets the world astir,
While slowly fades away the night
And shape and shadow blur

There is a time that's in-between
Our consciousness and sleep
When yet our dreams can still be seen
And we peer into the deep

That is the time when we can hear
Our angel softly call,
Softly for he's standing near,
"Rise again after your fall."

Every Morning a Masterpiece

Every morning a masterpiece
Greets my waking eye
On the canvas above the world
Spread across the sky

Where The Maker's boundless beauties
Make men stop and stare
And wonder that He should make this
World with so much care

"The heavens are telling the glory of God . . . the firmament proclaims His handiwork." Psalm 19, 1

Note on *In a Night Grown Cold*

A Lily as a Symbol: Tradition holds that when the angel Gabriel came to Our Lady at The Annunciation, he bore in his hand a lily to symbolize Our Lady's purity.

Isaiah's Line: Tradition also says that Our Lady was reading Scripture at the time of The Annunciation, and that the angel Gabriel appeared at the exact moment Our Lady read Isaiah's line:

"Behold, a virgin shall conceive and bear a Son . . ."
Isaiah 7, 14. Thus Our Lady is often depicted with a
book in images of The Annunciation.

Historical image depicting Belgrade in 1456

By a Miraculous Victory: As a vast Muslim
horde invaded Europe the Pope ordered all
Christians to pray The Angelus (see page 46 for the
prayer) for victory, three times a day, and ordered
church bells throughout Christendom to ring every
morning, noon, and night, to call the faithful to The
Angelus prayer. The Muslim army, with more than
160,000 soldiers, came against the small Christian
outpost of Belgrade, which had only about 5,000
men, drawn from many nations. It seemed a
hopeless cause, yet the 5,000 resisted, and
incredibly The Muslims were held back. Held

back, but still they continued their assault. Finally, with the fortress of Belgrade battered to pieces by shelling, the Muslims broke inside the city gates. At that moment, a great army of Christian peasants led by Saint John of Capistrano came chanting the name of Jesus and charged the Muslim horde. The peasants had no swords, no spears, no cannons, no armor, no horses—only sticks, stones, and farm implements. But a miracle occurred. As the Christians attacked, chanting the name of Jesus, terror struck the Muslims and they fled in panic. The Christians pursued and achieved complete victory, saving all of Europe from the Muslim invasion.

King Canute has his throne brought to the seashore and commands the tide to recede

Who Commands the Wind and Sea: In Scripture God reveals Himself through His mastery of wind and sea. God makes "the storm be still, and the waves of the sea . . . hushed." Ps 107, 29; Job 26, 11-14; Ps 89, 9.   So when the great conqueror King Canute was flattered by his courtiers as being a god, he had his throne taken to the edge of the sea and he commanded the tide to recede. When the tide did not obey, it proved that Canute was not a god. But when Jesus commanded the waves and wind, they obeyed Him. Mk 4, 35-41; Mt 8, 23-27; Lk 8, 22-24. Thus the disciples asked: "Who then is this, that even the wind and sea obey Him?" Mk 4, 41.

Jesus stilling the storm on the Sea of Galilee

In a Night Grown Cold

The cawing of crows in a night grown cold
In deepening dusk when the bells have
tolled

For The Angelus Prayer of Gabriel
Who came to Our Lady in Israel

Bearing a lily as a sign
As Our Lady read Isaiah's line

For still this prayer commemorates
How after the foe had broken the gates

By miracle a victory came
Through the power of The Holy Name

When peasants bearing sticks and staves
Chanted the name of God Who saves

In the fields beyond the broken walls
And splintered lintels of Belgrade's halls

Where the foe in droves into the dust,
Before the peasant's battle lust,

Fell to men who had no sword
But called upon the name of the Lord

And still today the bells are rung
And the prayer is said in every tongue

In thanks and prayer for victory
To the God Who commands the wind and sea

Who always rules in every land
And holds us each within His hand

The Angelus Prayer

The traditional times for the Angelus Bells and prayer are 6 AM, noon, and 6 PM. The prayer is said standing, with a genuflection at the words "And the word was made flesh/And dwelt among us." The prayer is as follows:

V: The angel of the Lord declared unto Mary,

R: And she conceived by the Holy Spirit.

Now recite the Hail Mary.

V: Behold the handmaid of the Lord,

R: Be it done unto me according to thy word.

Recite a second Hail Mary.

V: And The Word was made flesh,

R: And dwelt among us.

Recite a third Hail Mary.

V: Pray for us, O Holy Mother of God,

R: That we may be made worthy of the promises of Christ.

Let us pray: Pour forth, we beseech Thee, O Lord, Thy grace into our hearts, that we to whom the Incarnation of Christ, Thy Son, was made known by the message of an angel, may by His Passion and Cross be brought to the glory of His Resurrection, through the same Christ, Our Lord, amen.

St. Mary's Church, Blymhill, Stratfordshire

Note on March 25th

Tradition says that The Annunciation occurred on March 25th, and that the Crucifixion of Jesus Christ also occurred on March 25th. Thus, Jesus entered this world on the same day He left it.

The Twenty-Fifth Day of March

The Twenty-Fifth day of March
Remember, all ye men
For on this day your God and King
To the womb did enter in

The womb of Our Blessed Lady
Who Gabriel came to see
With The Annunciation
Of the miracle that could be

When she would be overshadowed
And conceive within her womb
The Son of the Living God
Bound from birth unto the tomb

For upon that same day again
A shadow would fall upon the world
When beneath a piece of parchment
Where nailed to The Cross it curled

The Son conceived upon this day
On this same day would die
Like a serpent made of bronze
Lifted up into the sky

When on the parchment men would see
The words written above his head,
"This is the King of the Jews,"
In three tongues the words all read

Until beneath the shadow
That on them fell that day
The letters at last no man could see
To discern what they might say

But Longinus the Centurion
Even in the dark could see
And: "This was surely the Son of God,"
Aloud to the world said he

When that day overshadowed
Our King came down from His throne
To be borne into the dark
Within the tomb of stone

For the Twenty-Fifth day of March,
For man's emancipation,
Our King would complete the journey
Begun on The Annunciation

And from the cave of Bethlehem
From the manger made of wood
To the tomb newly hewn of stone
By His side Our Lady stood

For on this day the miracle
That Gabriel said could be
Came to pass at Our Lady's word,
Be it done so unto me

Note on *He Saw the Promise from Afar*

Each Child Shining Like a Star: The Lord took Abraham outside and said: "Look toward heaven, and number the stars, if you are able . . . so shall your descendants be." Genesis 15, 5.

The Child of Laughter: God told Abraham that he would have a son by his wife Sarah, and Abraham "fell on his face and laughed, and said to himself, 'Shall a child be born to a man who is a hundred years old? Shall Sarah, who is ninety years old, bear a child?'" Genesis 17, 17. But God said to Abraham: ". . . Sarah your wife shall bear you a son, and you shall call his name Isaac." Genesis 17, 19.

The Three Who Came: "And the Lord appeared to [Abraham] by the Oaks of Mamré, as he sat at the door of his tent in the heat of the day. [Abraham] lifted up his eyes and looked, and behold, three men stood in front of him." Genesis 18, 1-2. Abraham prepared a meal for The Three "and he stood by them under the tree while they ate." Genesis 18, 8. And God told Abraham again, there beneath the Oaks of Mamré, that Sarah would bear him a son, and now it was Sarah who laughed when she heard, and God asked why Sarah had laughed, saying: "Is anything too hard for the Lord? At the appointed time I will return to you, in the spring, and Sarah shall have a son." Genesis 18, 14.

The Boy Who Now Carried the Wood: ". . . Abraham took the wood of the burnt offering, and laid it on Isaac his son . . . So they went both of them together." Genesis 22, 6.

Mount Moriah: Scripture (2 Chron 3:1) and tradition tell us that Mount Moriah, the place of

Abraham's sacrifice of Isaac, was the same place where the Temple of Jerusalem would one day be built. Further, Isaac was a grown man at the time of sacrifice, so must have consented to be bound and to serve as the sacrifice. Isaac carried the wood of his own sacrifice up to the mountain where he would be a voluntary sacrificial victim, thus prefiguring Christ. See notes to Genesis Chapter 22 in the Ignatius Catholic Study Bible.

He Saw the Promise From Afar

He saw the promise from afar:
Each child shining like a star

Spangling all the heavens vast
Their radiance in darkness cast

Even treading up the slopes
Of Mount Moriah with all his hopes

In the child of laughter at his side
Born of Sarah, his beloved bride

For did not They say beside his tent,
The Three Who came, before They went,

"For God Who called you out to go,"
"To this Promised Land you did not know,"

"All things are possible, as you shall see,"
"Who stand beside Us now beneath this tree,"

"In Spring We shall return once more,"
"Here where you sat beside your door,"

"And Sarah then shall laugh for joy,"
"As she holds her first born baby boy."

And he, too, Abraham well understood,
The boy who now carried the wood,

The son The Three to him foretold,
One day in his arms again would hold

And though on Mount Moriah he could not see
How it was that this should be

Yet still he held in his memory
Words he heard once at the Oaks of Mamré

As up the slope with his son he trod:
"All things are possible with God."

The Sun and the Sea

I sit in the shade beneath a tree
In the summertime beside the sea
And watch the sparkles on the bay
Where sun and sea together play

I am the sun and you are the sea
Come and sit in the shade with me
And together sparkle like the bay
When sun and sea together play

Providence, Rhode Island, circa 1910

Note on *From a Child's Birth*

Meeting Rebekah at the well. Genesis 24, 15.

Jacob born to Rebekah: Abraham charged his trusted servant to find a wife for Isaac from among Abraham's own people in the land of

Mesopotamia. When the servant found Rebekah, he gave her a ring of gold. Rebekah married Isaac, but Rebekah was barren. Isaac prayed to the Lord for Rebekah, after which Rebekah conceived and bore their twin sons, Esau and Jacob. Genesis, chapters 24 & 25. Many miracles are associated with Jacob, including the vision of Jacob's Ladder.

Jacob sees his future wife Rachel at the well. Genesis 29, 9-11.

Joseph the man who saw in dreams:
Laban, the brother of Rebekah (Jacob's mother), and thus Jacob's uncle, was the father of Rachel. Laban schemed against Jacob and tricked him, using Jacob's love for Rachel as the lure to trap Jacob into fourteen years of service. But Jacob eventually married Rachel and gained his freedom from Laban. It is from Jacob, whom God renames Israel, that the twelve tribes of Israel descend, and from the union of Jacob and Rachel, who up to then was barren, that Joseph is born. Genesis, chapters 29, 30, 31, 35. Joseph was given visions of prophecy in dreams and the ability to interpret dreams. By this ability he saved Egypt from starvation, and in the process also saved the sons of Jacob, the great famine came. Genesis, chapters 37, 39-47.

Moses in the basket.

Moses drawn from the Nile's water:
Pharoah commanded that every male Hebrew child
be killed by being cast into the Nile. The mother of
Moses placed Moses in a basket daubed with pitch
and bitumen, and set him afloat on the Nile.
Pharoah's daughter found the basket and kept
Moses as her own son, thus saving his life. Exodus,
chapters 1 & 2.

The angel comes to Samson's mother with the annunciation of Samson's birth, Segovia Cathedral

Samson born when an angel came: An unnamed angel came to an unnamed woman in a field and told her she would bear a son who would be a Nazarite dedicated to the Lord from birth and who would begin to deliver Israel from the Philistines. This would be a miraculous birth, since the woman was barren. The angel came again and told both the woman and her husband, Manoah, "it is wonderful," and Manoah and his wife offered a burnt offering and cereal offering to The Lord "Who works wonders". The son was born as the angel foretold, and his parents named him Samson. Judges, chapter 13.

Hannah, Samuel's mother, prays silently in the temple. 1 Samuel, chapter 1

Samuel, the son of the silent prayer:
Hannah was barren and prayed to the Lord a silent

prayer that she might have a son, and she vowed
that if she did, her son would be a Nazarite
dedicated to the service of the Lord from his birth.
The Lord granted Hannah's prayer, and the son she
bore was Samuel. Samuel, chapter 1.

John the Baptist who leapt for joy:
Elizabeth, who was a cousin of Our Lady, was
barren and advanced in age. The angel Gabriel
came to Elizabeth's husband, Zechariah, while he

ministered in The Temple of the Lord. Gabriel told
Zechariah that Elizabeth would conceive and bear a
son who would be great in the sight of the Lord,
and that the son should be named John. This came
to pass, and then, sixth months after John's
conception, the angel Gabriel came to Our Lady to
tell her she would be the mother of God, and
informed her of Elizabeth's miraculous pregnancy.
After Jesus was conceived within Our Lady's womb,
Our Lady went with haste to the hill country of
Judea to visit Elizabeth. Upon hearing the voice of
Our Lady raised in greeting, John the Baptist leapt
for joy within the womb of his mother Elizabeth.
Luke, chapter 1.

Simeon holds the Christ Child, from St. Brendan's
Cathedral, Loughren, Ireland

From a Child's Birth

What is this lesson that we've been taught
In the number of miracles God has
wrought

In bringing blessings to this Earth
Coming from a child's birth

Isaac born to Sarah when she was old
And Jacob to Rebekah with her ring of gold

And Joseph, the man who saw in dreams,
Born to Rachel of Laban's schemes

Moses drawn from the Nile's water
Even by the Pharoah's daughter

Samson born when an angel came
In a field to a woman never named

Samuel, the son of the silent prayer
Of Hannah, his mother, in her despair

And John the Baptist who leapt for joy
When still in the womb Elizabeth carried her boy

And Mary's Son Who sacrificed
For us Himself: Jesus Christ

Note on *Mary Magdalen*

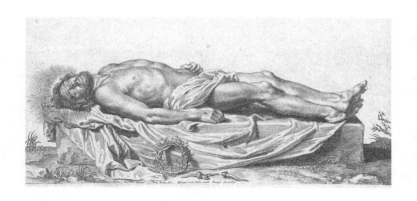

When Mary Magdalen faced toward the tomb: Mary Magdalen was at The Crucifixion (Mark 15, 40) and watched when the body of Jesus was taken down and carried to the tomb. She sat opposite the tomb (Matthew 27, 61) and watched as Jesus was laid in the tomb (Mark 15, 47).

The day the light had gone out from the sky: At Jesus' Crucifixion, the sun went dark for three hours, from noon to 3 P.M., while Jesus hung on The Cross. Matthew 27, 45; Mark 15, 33; Luke 23, 44-45. The earth shook, the veil in the temple was torn in two, tombs were opened, the bodies of saints were raised, and saints appeared to people throughout Jerusalem. Matthew 27, 51-53; Mark 15, 38; Luke 23, 45.

Tears that from her pierced heart had welled . . . The feet of Him . . . you again shall hold: According to tradition Mary Magdalen is the woman who washed the feet of Christ with her tears and dried his feet with her hair. Luke 7, 36-50; John 12, 1-8. After His resurrection, Mary Magdalen met Jesus in The Garden where His tomb was located, and fell at His feet and held His feet again. Matthew 28, 9.

She who had anointed Him . . . Breaker of the Alabaster Jar: Tradition also tells us that Mary Magdalen was the woman who anointed

Christ with pure spikenard from the alabaster jar. Mark 14, 3-9; Matthew 26, 6-13; Luke 7, 36-50; John 12, 1-8. Christ said: "She has done a beautiful thing to me . . . wherever this gospel is preached in the whole world, what she has done will be told in memory of her." Matthew 26, 10 & 13.

A man like lightning: When Mary
Magdalen came with other women to the tomb on
the third day, which was a Sunday, the first day of
the week, she saw a man like lightning—
presumably an angel—perched on the stone which
had been rolled away from the entrance to the
tomb. The angel told them that Jesus was risen.
Matthew 28, 2-10. The angel also commanded
Mary Magdalen to tell the disciples that Jesus had
risen. Matthew 28, 7. Saint Thomas Aquinas noted
that as it was a woman who announced the words

of death to man, so at The Resurrection it was a woman who announced the word of life to man.

As in The Garden He has called before: Jesus in The Garden recalls Genesis. In The Garden of Eden God walked with Adam and Eve until Adam and Eve turned away from God and chose sin and death over grace and life. Then Adam and Eve hid themselves in The Garden rather than meeting God in The Garden. Now, after the death and resurrection of Jesus, whereby Jesus paid the debt of man's sin and repaired the great rift in Creation caused by sin at The Fall, God again walks in The Garden, and now His children, rather than hiding from Him, once again meet Him in The Garden. Now, instead of The Fall into sin, God's children fall at the feet of their Lord and Savior. Matthew 28, 9.

When Mary Magdalen Faced Toward the Tomb

When Mary Magdalen faced toward the
    tomb
    The most terrible day the world has
known,
The day that Jesus died to lift our doom,
And His body was laid behind the stone

That day the light had gone out from the sky
Power shook the Earth that men might fear it
And from The Cross men heard their Savior cry
When for them He yielded up His spirit

On that day were opened tombs, old and new,
And the bodies of saints asleep were raised
And the temple curtain was torn in two
And The Magdalen faced toward His tomb and
gazed

Feet that once had walked the sea's heaving swell
She who had anointed Him now beheld
Wrapped in a shroud and pierced where once there
fell
Her own tears that from her pierced heart had
welled

But Breaker of the Alabaster Jar,
Not all of this story has yet been told
The feet of Him for Whom shone Jacob's Star
Shall walk again and you again shall hold

When there comes the morning of the third day
A man like lightning shall come to meet you
At the tomb where the stone is rolled away
And perched upon the stone he shall greet you

A message he will give for you to bear
As apostle to the Apostles who
By an angel given good news to share
Shall tell them how all things are made anew!

Yet there will at the tomb that day be more
For in The Garden you shall hear Him call
As in The Garden He has called before
That you, unhidden, at His feet might fall

The Patriarch Joseph, Ruler of Egypt for Pharoah

Joseph Asked Before He Died

Great Joseph, he, the mighty one,
Who stood astride the Nile
Hovered just this side of death
And spoke before its trial:

"Promise me before I die
My bones shall not remain
Within this land of servitude
Where once I gathered grain,"

"Grain that made the Pharoah strong
As with bread he forged a chain
Which I can see one day shall bind
Those who fled the drought of rain,"

"Yet still the grain that I preserved
God ordained for Jacob's sons
For from Abraham through Israel
His covenant still runs,"

"My father Jacob saw in dreams
And poured out oil on the stone
And wrestled with an angel when
Awaiting Esau all alone,"

Jacob's dream

Jacob wrestles with an angel

"The many-colored cloak he gave
To his son who dreamed as he
That dipped in blood broke his heart
When in slavery,"

"For shekels of silver that son was sold
By brothers who cast him in the pit
But God ordained that son one day
In authority to sit,"

"For God through trial fitted him
Like an arrow to the string
To do His will when came the time
His grace to Jacob's sons to bring,"

Joseph sold into slavery

"For well does Noah's Archer know
The bow and draw its string with might
And by His hand the arrow guides
Even as it speeds in flight,"

"His is the bow of many hues
As was the coat that I once wore
And He works through dreams and lowly things
In which men put little store,"

"I have seen His bow span the sky
And I have known in life His grace
And now I go to journey on
At last to see His face,"

"I have also seen the day will come
When forth from this land of toil
God will lead out Israel
Bearing Egypt's spoil,"

Joseph's dream

"Bear also away my bones that day
To where in my vision gleams
The land which since my bondage day
I have seen always in my dreams,"

"Across the Jordan let them go
To where the Oaks of Mamré stand
With my fathers at last to rest
Within The Promised Land."

Joseph's body at his death in Egypt

The Panagia Tricherousa, "The All-Holy (a title of the Virgin Mary) with Three Hands" (the third hand, made of silver, was placed in the lower corner of the icon by Saint John of Damascus, in thanks for Our Lady's miraculous healing of his severed hand). The icon is presently located in Hilander Monastery on Mount Athos, Greece

Saint John of Damascus

Saint John of Damascus was born in Damascus around 645 A.D. A priest, monk, and writer of poetry, apologetics, and polemics, he is a Doctor of the Church known as "The Doctor of the Assumption" and, for his defense of images during the iconoclast heresy, "The Doctor of Christian Art."

However, as a truth-teller, Saint John's writings angered many powerful people. Their animosity ultimately led to a plot culminating in the severing of Saint John's writing hand by scimitar at the order of the Sultan of Damascus.

Cradling the bloody stump of his severed arm, Saint John prayed to Our Lady before the icon now known as The Panagia Tricherousa. He passed out while praying, then saw, as if in a dream, Our Lady come to him and heal his hand. As she healed him, Our Lady commanded Saint John to use his hand and writing gift in the service of Christ. Saint John awoke and found his hand fully restored.

In thanks, he had a silver hand made as a votive offering and affixed it to the icon before which he had prayed to Our Lady, thus adding the "third hand" to the "Three Handed" icon.

He died approximately 760 A.D.; his feast day is December 4. He is a patron saint of poets.

Saint John of Damascus, Patron Saint of Poets

To you, Saint John of Damascus,
Whose hand penned the lines
In praise Our Lady and her Son
Confounding the world's designs,

In the city of Damascus
That led to the Sultan's command
That the sharpened scimitar
Sever your writing hand

It was to you Our Lady came,
Whose praises you had sung,
For she willed still your words one day
Be read in every tongue

She healed your hand that held the pen
That you might write once more
That from your heart across the page
The words again might pour

The patron saint of poets,
Who Our Queen came to restore
By your life and work you show us
What the writing gift is for

Choir stall from the monastery church of Saints Peter and
Paul, Ravensburg, Baden-Wuerttemberg, Germany, depicting
Our Lady healing the hand of Saint John of Damascus

Note on Saint Cuthman

I first encountered the story of Saint Cuthman at Penfold's Field in Joseph Pearce's wonderful book *The Three Y's Men* (the story of a walking journey across Sussex in the company of three imaginary (or are they?) fellow pilgrims, one of whom bears a strikingly resemblance to the original Sussex rambler, Hilaire Belloc; Pearce's book makes a worthy addition to the tradition of Belloc's *The Four Men*). Pearce sent me searching for more information on Saint Cuthman. Of the several ancient lives of Cuthman written in Latin, one has been translated into English by a scholar named Roger Pearse, who posted his translation on-line for all to use.

It makes a fascinating read. Born around 681 A.D., Saint Cuthman was a commoner, the son of a shepherd. When Cuthman was still young his father died, casting he and his mother into poverty. They eventually lost their home and set out, wandering penniless across the land, searching for a place to live and a new start in life.

So perhaps Belloc is not the original Sussex rambler, but is himself a part of a tradition began long before he was born.

By the Saint Cuthman and his widowed mother commenced their wandering, Cuthman's mother was crippled, having lost the use of her legs. Because she could no longer walk, Saint Cuthman pulled her in a handcart as they ventured out alone into the world.

When they came to Penfold's Field, a group of people was out mowing the field, gathering a rich crop. The mowers saw Cuthman trudging across the countryside pulling his mother in a handcart and laughed at the ragged pair.

In response, Saint Cuthman said: "Laugh man, weep Heaven," and on the instant an inundation of rain poured out of a clear blue sky upon Penfold's Field, and Penfold's Field only. Those who moments before were harvesting the riches of the land and laughing at the misfortune of others were stunned into silence as all their crop was ruined.

Tradition says that ever since, it has rained on Penfold's Field every mowing day.

Many miracles are associated with Saint Cuthman. Once, when working as a shepherd, Cuthman needed to leave his sheep in the field. To ensure that they would not be lost or scattered, Cuthman traced a ring on the grass around his sheep with his staff. He then planted the staff in the middle of the ring and commanded the sheep not to cross the invisible line he had marked with his staff on the grass until he returned. Cuthman left, and the sheep obeyed him, remaining within the unseen circle until Cuthman returned and pulled his staff out of the ground again.

Another famous miracle can still be seen to this day: the church of Saint Andrew. Saint Cuthman felt called to build a church for God, a church dedicated to Saint Andrew. Cuthman began working on the church alone, though he had no experience or training in construction and no tools. Others saw the miracles occurring through Saint Cuthman, and heard his wonderous words when he spoke of God, and came to join him in his building project, and the church began to rise. Then, at a critical juncture, the main beam intended for the roof of the church was damaged by the amateur volunteers, rendering it useless.

The project seemed to have reached its end. They didn't know what to do or how to proceed.

At that moment, a stranger came along and offered to help. In a few minutes, the stranger was able to repair the beam and help Cuthman and his men put it into place. Amazed, Saint Cuthman asked: "Who are you?" The stranger replied: "I am he in whose name you are building this church," then vanished.

It was Saint Andrew himself. The church was completed and named the Church of Saint Andrew. It has since been renamed The Church of Saint Andrew and Saint Cuthman, and can still be seen and visited today in the Village of Steyning (though it has been expanded and renovated in the millennium and more since it was first constructed).

Saint Cuthman's feast day is February 8.

St. Andrew's, with the statue of St. Cuthman across the road

Saint Cuthman at Penfold's Field

66 "Laugh man, weep Heaven,"
Said aloud the saint
When at a widow's sorrow
They laughed without restraint

The sorrow of widows and the poor
They scorned and made their sport
Those in Penfold's Field who mowed
And feared not Heaven's court

But their laughter quickly faded
When from a sky of blue
Torrents of rain descended
To ruin the crop that grew

The bounty they had expected
All suddenly was gone
While the poor man who had spoken
Drew the widow on

The widow who was his mother
And crippled, no more could walk,
And her son who was a poor man
Pulled her handcart while they talked

Of the glories of their Maker
And the blessings from their God
Even while in poverty
A lonely road they trod

For he who was a poor man
Also was a saint
And bore the crosses he'd been given
In joy without complaint

And always filled with love for God
And the beauties of creation
Given freely as a gift
As was his own salvation

Saint Cuthman in the village Steyning
Built a church with his own hands
A shepherd who the sheep obeyed
When he gave to them commands

And at the words of this saint
The rains from Heaven fell
The laughter of the haughty
In their spoiled fields to quell

That in West Sussex men might learn
Wherein to place their joy
Not in the riches of the Earth
The moth might still destroy

But in those things eternal
For which Heaven laughs or cries
The things which are unchanging
Unlike our earthly skies

And still unto this very day
When Penfold's Field is mown
Rain descends like tears upon
Land cruel laughter once had sown

Statue of Saint Cuthman across the road from the
church he built, St. Andrew's, gazing at the church
in the village of Steyning

Baby Clothes

Baby cloths! I can't believe
There was ever an arm so small
To fit in such a tiny sleeve
But so began us all

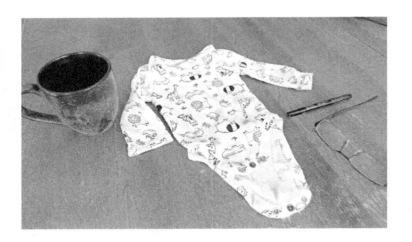

The Plan is His

In a moment all things can change
And circumstances rearrange

So what you saw ahead for you
Shifts suddenly to something new

For while it's true there is a plan,
A course our Lord plots for each man,

Remember that the plan is His
And seldom what you think it is

Compass Point Storm Tower, Cornwall, UK

Compass Point Storm Tower, Cornwall, UK
The Cardinal Points are carved on its walls

Note on *The Call of the Mower*

Winston Churchill at Whitehall, May 8, 1945, VE Day

The ever-Biblical Winston Churchill once said that war "was the normal occupation of man, and gardening." *Churchill, Walking with Destiny*, by Andrew Roberts, pg 255. From the beginning, as

Moses wrote in Genesis, God put man in the Garden "to till it and keep it." Genesis 2, 15. To till it: to work the land and produce its fruits. And to keep it: to defend it from enemies, to protect it, to defeat the wild beasts and monsters that would ruin and despoil it—like the dragon, the serpent, who entered The Garden to lie and tempt.

The sword and the plow: they have been man's calling and duty from the beginning: to protect and provide.

Churchill during World War II, flying from Virginia to Bermuda, 1942, on a round of war time conferences

The Call of the Mower

The call of the mower, loud and clear
Like a bee is buzzing in my ear

For since first in Eden shone the dawn
It's been Man's chore to mow the lawn

Before the first fig leaf was sewn
Man clipped and chopped at what was grown

Daily old Adam The Garden tended
Until his tenancy there was ended

And now at last it falls to me
To trim the hedges evenly

It's been said, and now I know,
That as you sow, so shall you mow!

The Gift of God to Man of Speech

The gift of God to Man of speech
Puts life or death within our reach

For by the power of the tongue
Can souls be won or come undone

The Future

I know not what the future holds
But I know it's in Your hands
So as its mystery unfolds
I'll trust it to Your plans

What a Strange Age It Is That's Ours

Hear the rumble of the engines
Feel the rattle of the plane
As breaking free of gravity
Metal wings and rivets strain

The ancient dream again to grasp,
The impossible defy,
As off we slip the binding clasp
And vault into the sky

What a strange age it is that's ours
Where men can soar into the sky
Higher than the cloudy towers
And never bat an eye

Why in this, an age of wonders,
Should now wonder cease in men?
So that into Babel's blunders
We're doomed to fall again

For are His wonders any less
When He works them through our clay?
If we could see we would confess
We see His wonders every day

Note on John Winthrop

Statue of John Winthrop at Boston's First Church,
Boston, Massachusetts

John Winthrop (1587-1649) was a Puritan
leader, the first governor of The Massachusetts Bay
Colony, and a founder of the city of Boston. It was
Winthrop who first said that America was a Biblical
"City on a Hill," shining for all to see, a light and
beacon of hope for mankind.

Of the many remarkable occurrences in
Winthrop's life, one is a famous incident of

Winthrop's Christian charity and the—seemingly—coincidental timing of events that sometimes reveal the hand of Divine Providence.

The colonists were busy upon their arrival in the New World clearing land and building homes. They could not put in a crop until the wilderness was cleared for farming, so initially they relied on food from the mother country to survive.

But the history of New World colonization was rife with tragedy resulting from long-expected ships that did not arrive on time. The delay of ships to Jamestown led to "The Starving Time," 1609-1610 A.D., when approximately 440 of the 500 people of Jamestown starved to death: about 90% of the entire population.

A time came when the residents of Boston also faced hunger as they waited on ships from England to bring them food. Would the ships come? Would they come on time?

While the people of Massachusetts waited and watched, their food stores ran lower and lower.

Finally, Winthrop was left with one loaf of bread baking in the oven and only a little flour remaining in his flour jar.

At that moment, a poor neighbor, who had nothing at all, came begging for food.

Not knowing when, or if, he would get food again, Winthrop gave away the last of his flour.

And then the intervention of Divine Providence was made known: at that very moment, the long awaited ships were spotted sailing into the bay!

John Winthrop's Flour

The oven held one loaf of bread
The last that he would eat
For fast away their flour sped
While waiting on the fleet

From England's green and fertile shores
From whence their grain would come
At last that they might fill their stores
And the pains of hunger numb

But no ships sailed into the bay
And each day they saw pass
Their flour ran on swift away
As sands through an hourglass

When history was written down
Would Boston see its name
One day remembered with Jamestown
For ships that never came

And The Starving Time that followed
When people died in scores
And their land with pits was hollowed
For graves along its shores

The future then he could not know,
When peering in his jar
He saw the flour drawn down low,
And felt England then afar

But the Shining City Upon the Hill
Must shine for men to see
 If as a spark in passing, still
A light eternally

What flour he had remaining
John Winthrop gave away
Thus through his want sustaining
His brothers another day

Then the hand of God they knew
For that very hour
They spied upon the ocean blue
Sails as white as flour!

At Harvest Time

At harvest time we gather in
And gathering remember when

The seeds were planted long ago
And thank the Lord Who made them grow

All the Fruits of Creation Their Glories Give

In Autumn time when atop the trees
The colors of fire are in the leaves

The Harvest Moon in the sky will shine
On pumpkins orange upon the vine

Apples are crisp and caramel is sweet
And cider is pressed and deer are fleet

And geese through the sky fly in a "V"
And sap flows brown from the maple tree

For making syrup and sugar soft
And hay is gathered in the barn's high loft

And the corn is ripe on stalks that sway
And dusk falls soon on All Saints Day

All the fruits of Creation their glories give
To the mighty God by Whom they live

It's Halloween Tonight

Ghosts in the trees bob on the breeze
It's Halloween tonight!
My old friend Jack is finally back
With a grin that's fiery bright

We'll pray for the souls of all of those
Who've died that we hold dear
For All Souls Day is on the way
It comes this time each year

So Trick or Treat! And candy we'll eat!
While Jack O' Lanterns glow
And the old black cat and the web-winged bat
Prowl as the night winds blow

And inky clouds surround the moon like shrouds
So it burns an aureole
Of silver light in the murky night
While round us the heavens roll

Over dry corn stalks that shake where there walks
Things hidden from our sight
And beyond the veil through the clouds they sail
It's Halloween tonight!

Genius in the Jumble

Through the snow away they go
The crazy tracks I see
Left by feet both small and fleet
When moving stealthily

In the night when by the light
Of moonshine's pearly glow
Small things thread with tiny tread
A zig-zag through the snow

Tracks the eye within can spy
Genius in the jumble
For owls that fly and foxes sly
The mouse thereby keeps humble

Earth's Baptismal Gown

No stars tonight the skies reveal
Wrapped in their snowy shawl
The clouds of snow the stars conceal
While snows in silence fall

The snows drift down like silent stars
Through winter's dark and cold
Spilled from Heaven's upended jars
Which silent snowfalls hold

The stars of snow through frosty air
Twirl while they tumble down
That Heaven with the Earth might share
A white baptismal gown

As from the winter shall arise,
When birds again will sing,
And flowers reach up toward the skies,
New life when comes the Spring

Like a Winking Eye

I saw in the sky
Like a winking eye
A crescent of moon appear

Through a gauzy cloud
As though through a shroud
Shimmer where the shroud was sheer

While down below
In the blowing snow
That the cloud cast on the wind

I winked in return
And thought I discerned
In its crescent the moon had grinned

What in the Darkness We Might Find

It's curious in the day
To see what passed at night
What moved about among us
Hidden from our sight

When upon new fallen snow
Their tracks reveal to us
The rambles of the creatures
That come out after dusk

And remind us that, though rarely seen,
And often far from mind,
We must take care still of what
In the darkness we might find

In Early Morning the Ice Aglow

In early morning the ice aglow
  With lustrous astral gleams
  From starlight descending down below
In shimmering silvery beams

On an ancient journey that began
Long millions of years ago
To cross the cosmos, vast in span,
At last to set the ice aglow

As when Jacob's Star that Balaam's eye
Beheld arising from afar
Shone in the dark Judean sky
As the wandering Christmas Star

So also will things beyond our ken,
From beyond our time and space,
Set in motion we know not when,
Light us within one day with Grace

Praise the Lord of Frost and Snow

When sunlight strikes the fields of frost
And makes the mist to rise
And fills it with its golden light
That pours from golden skies

So the earth itself seems aflame
As all is set aglow
Then praise the Lord of sun and flame
The Lord of frost and snow

Poems for Christmas

The Manger of Their Master Know

 pagan prophet told the sign
   By which the pagan kings would find
In a manger bed of straws
Who all the cosmos overawes

For with the shepherds also came,
Led by the light of Heaven's flame,

The Magi kings from afar
Who followed after Jacob's Star

For both the ox and ass, kneeling low,
The manger of their master know

Note on the Ox and Ass

Traditionally, the ox represents the gentiles and the ass represents the Jewish people. So at Christmas, both the gentiles and Jews—hence all people—are represented at The Nativity and bow at the manger of their Master and Maker.

Note on Balaam's Prophecy of Jacob's Star

It is a mistake to think that, in the cosmos-engulfing battle of good and evil, the fight is between believers and unbelievers.

It is not.

The great battle is between believers who choose the side of God, and believers who choose evil.

Read the Gospels. The demons believe. They have not the slightest doubt about the existence of God. They act not out of ignorance or misunderstanding or confusion.

They act out of evil.

They have chosen evil.

They hate.

So it was also in the Old Testament.

All the world saw what God did with Israel in Egypt, and trembled. Yet, many would not join God, despite what they knew. They chose to oppose God and God's chosen people.

When Israel came out of Egypt, the pagan kings of the Holy Land sent for the pagan prophet Balaam to come and curse Israel, offering him extravagant riches to do so.

Balaam came, and three times tried to curse Israel, but each time, God instead put words of blessing for Israel into the mouth of Balaam.

Balaam himself prophesied Israel's triumph, and that from Israel would come a blessing for all nations, saying of Israel: "Blessed be everyone who blesses you, and cursed be every one who curses you." Numbers 24, 9.

Balaam also implored God to make him like Israel, saying: "Let me die the death of the righteous, and let my end by like his!" Numbers 23, 10.

Balaam said: "Water shall flow from his buckets, and his seed shall be in many waters, his king shall be higher than Agag, and his kingdom shall be exalted." Numbers 23, 10.

Of the might of Israel, of the coming power that would manifest itself through Israel, Balaam prophesied:

"God brings him out of Egypt;
He has as it were the horns of the wild ox,
He shall eat up the nations his adversaries,
And shall break their bones in pieces,
And pierce them through with his arrows.
He lurked, he lay down like a lion, and like a lioness; who will rouse him up?"

Numbers 24, 8-9

Yet Balaam in the end chose to side with the powers of the world against Israel! And as a result Balaam died by the sword of Israel. Joshua 13, 22.

The same drama plays out at Christmas. The Light comes into the world, but some men "loved darkness rather than light." John 3, 19. Jesus comes with a sword (Matthew 10, 34), to divide the good from the evil (Luke 12, 51), He is a sign and a contradiction destined for the rise and fall of many (Luke 2, 34-35).

Some rejoice, like the angels, the shepherds in the fields, and the Magi.

Others fear, and hate, and kill. Like Herod.

And Herod quakes for one more, very particular reason: Herod was an Edomite. He had been put in place as king over Israel by Rome, and Herod read the words of the prophet Balaam and, as his subsequent acts show, Herod believed, and Herod feared. Because Balaam also said, in prophesying the coming of the ultimate King Who would arise out of Israel:

> I see Him, but not now;
> I behold Him, but not near:
> A Star shall come forth out of Jacob,
> And a scepter shall rise out of Irael;
> It shall crush the forehead of Moab,
> And break down all the sons of Sheth.
> Edom shall be dispossessed,
> Seir also, His enemies, shall be dispossessed,
> While Israel does valiantly.

By Jacob shall dominion be exercised,
And the survivors of cities be destroyed!

Numbers 24, 17-19

A star is the sign of a royal birth, the birth of a king. A scepter is the sign of royal power.
That power is coming, and Edom shall be disposed.

Balaam beholding Jacob's Star

Jacob's Star Portends

Jacob's Star, Balaam said,
   Would signal at its rising
   From afar now had sped
The coming of the High King

So while Wise Men came from far away
And shepherds heard the call
Of angels' song on Christmas day
Herod trembled in his hall

For beheld from the height
Balaam saw from far away
To the world would come a might
Born on Christmas day

For the King the Star foretold
With scepter in His hand
One day would all dominion hold
And crush His foes in every land

Shepherds of the Paschal Lamb

When the shepherds kept their watch
Over flocks in fields by night
In the time when lambs were born
They beheld a wondrous sight

For the angels came to those
Who were tending to the fold
That shepherds of the paschal lamb
Be the first men to be told

That The Lamb of God was born
And by this, the angels said,
Know as the Christ the Child Who
In a manger lays His head.

Our Lady holding Jesus, St. Henry Catholic Church, St. Henry, Ohio

When Want the Land Enfolds

When the branches of trees are tipped in
    frost
    And shimmer with silvery light
While dark the winter skies are crossed
By the wings of crows in flight

And howls the wind through a glowering sky
With a gray and brooding mien
As hunger drives the crows to fly
Through a land that's now grown lean

Then through the cold and the biting wind
Like the shimmering of ice there gleams
A vision of hope for men who've sinned
That the prophets saw in dreams

For then does Christmas come at last
When want the land enfolds
And all the Glory of Heaven is cast
In the Baby Our Lady holds

Epiphany Prayer

O angel of the Christmas Star,
Bless us all, near and far,
Bless us here within our home
And wherever it is that we may roam

Guiding Wise Men by Its Rays

The Christmas Star shone through the night
To guide The Wise Men by its light

And from that first of Christmas days
It's guided wise men by its rays

To the manger in the stable where
Our Lord was born a baby bare

The Last Night of the Christmas Tree

The last night of the Christmas tree
And all the house asleep but me

The colored lights softly glow
That tomorrow in their bin we'll stow

For after passes The Epiphany
Down will come the Christmas Tree

Though in our hearts through the year
Its memory will bring us cheer

Until the year rolls round again
To the blessed month at its end

When our family once more will be
Blessed with grace from a Christmas Tree

For God so loved the world that He gave His only-begotten Son, that whoever believes in Him should not perish but have eternal life.

John 3, 16

Image Credits

https://commons.wikimedia.org/wiki/File:Schnorr_von_Carolsfeld
_Bibel_in_Bildern_1860_006.png; Author: Julis Schnorr von
Carolsfeld; License: Public Domain; Date: circa 1855

Pg. 16: Jesus enters Jerusalem; From
www.commons.wikimedia.org; URL:
https://commons.wikimedia.org/wiki/File:The_Bible_panorama,_o
r_The_Holy_Scriptures_in_picture_and_story_(1891)_(145983695
49).jpg; Author: William A. Foster; License: no known copyright
restrictions Domain; Date: 1891; image modified

Pg. 18: Storm in clouds; From www.commons.wikimedia.org; URL:
https://commons.wikimedia.org/wiki/File:Earth,_Venus_and_Jupit
er.jpg; Author: Manols Thravalos; License: Creative Commons
Attribution-Share Alike 4.0 International; Date: 21 October 2015

Pg. 19: Giants hurling stones; From www.commons.wikimedia.org;
URL: https://commons.wikimedia.org/wiki/File:Michel_Dorigny_-
_Gigantomachy,_after_Vouet,_1841,1211.39.93.jpg; Author:
Michel Dorigny; License: Public Domain; Date: 1841; image
modified

Pg. 20: Sunset; From www.commons.wikimedia.org; URL:
https://commons.wikimedia.org/wiki/File:Stringy_pink_and_orang
e_clouds_at_sunset_in_the_dry_paddy_fields_of_Don_Det_Laos.j
pg; Author: Basile Morin; License: Creative Commons Attribution-
Share Alike 4.0 International; Date: 30 October 2019; image
modified

Pg. 21: Adam and Eve clothing selves with Fig Leaves; From
www.commons.wikimedia.org; URL:
ttps://commons.wikimedia.org/wiki/File:The_Phillip_Medhurst_Pi
cture_Torah_20._Adam_%26_Eve_clothe_themselves._Genesis_ca
p_3_v_7._Sperling.jpg; Author: Phillip Medhurst; License: Creative
Commons Attribution-Share Alike 3.0 Unreported; Date: 1 January
2000; image modified

Pg. 23: Prairie; From www.commons.wikimedia.org; URL: From
www.commons.wikimedia.org; URL:
https://commons.wikimedia.org/wiki/File:June_2006_rain_on_the
prairie(0577e1ea-8448-4378-af63-74b6f60edeb3).jpg; Author:
National Park Service; License: Public Domain; Date: June 2006;
image modified

Pg. 24: Storm clouds on the sea; From
www.commons.wikimedia.org; URL:
https://commons.wikimedia.org/wiki/File:Lightning_storm_over_t
he_Caribbean.jpg; Author: Keith Pomakis; License: Creative
Commons Attribution-Share Alike 2.5 Generic; Date: 1913; image
modified

Pg. 26: Sunrise over the Earth seen from space; From
www.commons.wikimedia.org; URL:
https://commons.wikimedia.org/wiki/File:Cropped_Earth_with_Su

nburst.PNG; Author: NASA; License: Public Domain; Date: 1996; image modified

Pg. 27: Bright line of the horizon from the rising sun; From www.commons.wikimedia.org; URL: https://commons.wikimedia.org/wiki/File:NASA_astronaut_Scott_Kelly_captured_this_sunrise_over_the_US_East_Coast_04.jpg; Author: NASA; License: Public Domain; Date: 2016; image modified

Pg. 28: Moon rise over the Earth; From www.commons.wikimedia.org; URL: https://commons.wikimedia.org/wiki/File:Full_moon_partially_obscured_by_atmosphere.jpg; Author: NASA; License: Public Domain; Date: 1999; image modified

Pg. 29: Eagle; From www.commons.wikimedia.org; URL: https://commons.wikimedia.org/wiki/File:Haliaeetus_leucocephalus_in_flight_over_KSC.jpg; Author: NASA; License: Public Domain; Date: 6 September 2006; image modified

Pg. 31: Crow in flight; From www.commons.wikimedia.org; URL: https://commons.wikimedia.org/wiki/File:Jungle_crow_(Corvus_macrorhynchos)_from_anaimalai_hills_in_flight_JEG3217.jpg; Author: P Jeganathan; License: Creative Commons Attribution-Share Alike 4.0 International; Date: 7 July 2012; image modified

Pg. 32: Ship; From www.commons.wikimedia.org; URL: https://commons.wikimedia.org/wiki/File:NS_-_Pride_of_Baltimore_II.jpg; Author: Wladyslaw; License: Creative Commons Attribution-Share Alike 3.0 Unreported; Date: 21 September 2008; image modified

Pg. 33: Potipher's wife grasps Joseph's cloak; From www.commons.wikimedia.org; URL: https://commons.wikimedia.org/wiki/File:Schnorr_von_Carolsfeld_Joseph_and_Potiphar%27s_Wife.png; Author: Julis Schnorr von Carolsfeld; License: Public Domain; Date: 1860; image modified

Pg. 34: Joseph interprets Pharoah's dream; From www.commons.wikimedia.org; URL: https://commons.wikimedia.org/wiki/File:Foster_Bible_Pictures_0052-1_Joseph_Explains_the_King%27s_Dreams.jpg; Author: Bible Illustrations and What They Teach Us by Charles Foster; License: Public Domain; Date: 1897; image modified

Pg. 35: Joseph rules Egypt; From www.commons.wikimedia.org; URL: https://commons.wikimedia.org/wiki/File:Foster_Bible_Pictures_0052-2_Joseph_Is_Dressed_in_Beautiful_Clothes_and_Is_Riding_in_a_Chariot.jpg; Author: Bible Illustrations and What They Teach Us by Charles Foster; License: Public Domain; Date: 1897; image modified

Pg. 37: Baruch writes Jeremiah's prophecies; From www.commons.wikimedia.org; URL: https://commons.wikimedia.org/wiki/File:123.Baruch_Writes_Jeremiah%27s_Prophecies.jpg; Author: Gustave Dore; License: Public Domain; Date: 1866; image modified

Pg. 38: Angel waking man; From www.commons.wikimedia.org; URL: https://commons.wikimedia.org/wiki/File:Angel_Appearing_to_Sleeping_Shepherd_MET_181054.jpg; Author: Unknown; License: Public Domain; Date: 1700's; image modified

Pg. 39: Sunrise over the Jefferson Memorial; From www.commons.wikimedia.org; URL: https://commons.wikimedia.org/wiki/File:Con00313_(27661851820).jpg; Author: NOAA; License: Public Domain; Date: 7 February 2015; image modified

Pg. 40: The Annunciation; From www.commons.wikimedia.org; URL: https://commons.wikimedia.org/wiki/File:Schnorr_von_Carolsfeld_Bibel_in_Bildern_1860_162.png; Julis Schnorr von Carolsfeld; License: Public Domain; Date: 1860; image modified

Pg. 41: Belgrade in 1456; From www.commons.wikimedia.org; URL: https://commons.wikimedia.org/wiki/File:Kriechisch_Wyssenburg.jpg; Author: Sebastian Munster; License: Public Domain; Date: 1545; image modified

Pg. 42: King Canute issuing command to the tide; From www.commons.wikimedia.org; URL: https://commons.wikimedia.org/wiki/File:055-Canute_reproving_flattery_of_his_Courtiers.png; Author: John Cassell; License: Public Domain; Date: circa 1860; image modified

Pg. 43: Christ stilling the storm; From www.commons.wikimedia.org; URL: https://commons.wikimedia.org/wiki/File:%22Christ_stilling_the_tempest%22_-_painted_by_James_Hamilton_;_engraved_by_Samuel_Sartain,_Phila._LCCN2006677468.jpg; Author: James Hamilton; License: Public Domain; Date: 1867; image modified

Pg. 45: Sky; From www.commons.wikimedia.org; URL: https://commons.wikimedia.org/wiki/File:Sunset_with_trees_2.jpg; Author: W. Carter; License: Public Domain; Date: 7 April 2017; image modified

Pg. 47: St. Mary's church; From www.commons.wikimedia.org; URL: https://commons.wikimedia.org/wiki/File:Church_print_1797_vestry.jpg; Author: photo by James Loach of image by unknown artist; License: Public Domain; Date: October 2008 photo of 1797 print;

image modified

Pg. 48: Good Friday; From www.commons.wikimedia.org; URL: https://commons.wikimedia.org/wiki/File:Currier_Crucifixion_of_C hrist.jpg; Author: Nathanial Currier; License: Public Domain; Date: 1849; image modified

Pg. 51: The Annunciation; From www.commons.wikimedia.org; URL: https://commons.wikimedia.org/wiki/File:Annunciatie,_RP-P-BI-2441.jpg; Author: Gerard Seghers; License: Public Domain; Date: Circa 1600; image modified

Pg. 52: Abraham gazing at the stars; From www.commons.wikimedia.org; URL: https://commons.wikimedia.org/wiki/File:The_Phillip_Medhurst_P icture_Torah_89._Abraham%27s_Vision._Genesis_cap_15_v_5._Fr ederich.jpg; Author: Phillip Medhurst; License: Creative Commons Attribution-Share Alike 3.0 Unreported; Date: 1 January 2000; image modified

Pg. 53: Abraham greets The Three; From www.commons.wikimedia.org; https://commons.wikimedia.org/wiki/File:Foster_Bible_Pictures_0 027-1.jpg; Author: Unknown; License: Public Domain; Date: 1897; image modified

Pg. 54: The Three speak with Abraham; From www.commons.wikimedia.org; URL: https://commons.wikimedia.org/wiki/File:Foster_Bible_Pictures_0 029-1.jpg; Author: Unknown; License: Public Domain; Date: 1897; image modified

Pg. 55: Issac carries the wood; From www.commons.wikimedia.org; URL: https://commons.wikimedia.org/wiki/File:Fran%C3%A7ois_Torteb at_Prelude_to_the_sacrifice_of_Isaac,_who_carries_firewood_on_ his_shoulders_urged_on_by_his_father_at_left,_at_right_two_me n,_one_holding_a_donkey,_discuss_Isaac%27s_fate,_after_Vouet. _1665,_1841,1211.39.3.jpg; Author: Simon Vouet; License: Public Domain; Date: Circa 1600; image modified

Pg. 56: The angel stays Abraham's hand; From www.commons.wikimedia.org; URL: https://commons.wikimedia.org/wiki/File:Schnorr_von_Carolsfeld _Bibel_in_Bildern_1860_028.png; Author: Julis Schnorr von Carolsfeld; License: Public Domain; Date: Circa 1855; image modified

Pg. 58: Abraham and Isaac ascending the mountain of sacrifice; From www.commons.wikimedia.org; URL: https://commons.wikimedia.org/wiki/File:016.The_Testing_of_Abr aham%27s_Faith.jpg; Author: Gustave Dore; License: Public Domain; Date: 1866; image modified

Pg. 59: Providence, RI, tree beside the sea; From: URL:

142

https://commons.wikimedia.org/wiki/File:Providence_-
_the_sovthern_gateway_of_New_England,_provd_of_its_honorab
le_history,_happy_in_its_present_prosperity,_confident_of_its_fvt
vre_(1910)_(14761004416).jpg; Author: Henry Ames Barker; Date:
1910; License: No Known Copyright Restrictions; image modified
Pg. 60: Meting Rebekah at the well; From
www.commons.wikimedia.org; URL:
https://commons.wikimedia.org/wiki/File:The_Bible_panorama,_o
r_The_Holy_Scriptures_in_picture_and_story_(1891)_(148047411
13).jpg; Author: William A. Foster, The Bible Panorama; License:
No known copyright restrictions; Date: 1891; image modified
Pg. 61: Rachel at the well; From www.commons.wikimedia.org;
URL:
https://commons.wikimedia.org/wiki/File:The_Bible_panorama,_o
r_The_Holy_Scriptures_in_picture_and_story_(1891)_(147817482
51).jpg; Author: William A. Foster, The Bible Panorama; License:
No known copyright restrictions; Date: 1891; image modified
Pg. 62: Moses in the basket; From www.commons.wikimedia.org;
URL:
https://commons.wikimedia.org/wiki/File:Foster_Bible_Pictures_0
059-1_Moses_Floating_on_the_Water.jpg; Author: Louis-Pierre
Henrique Dupont in Bible Pictures and What They Teach Us by
Charles Foster; License: Public Domain; Date: 1897; image
modified
Pg. 63: Pharaoh's daughter and the finding of Moses; From
www.commons.wikimedia.org; URL:
https://commons.wikimedia.org/wiki/File:Foster_Bible_Pictures_0
007-1.jpg; Author: from Bible Pictures and What They Teach Us by
Charles Foster; License: Public Domain; Date: 1897; image
modified
Pg. 64: Annunciation to Samson's unnamed mother; From
www.commons.wikimedia.org; URL:
https://commons.wikimedia.org/wiki/File:Hazelelponi_y_el_%C3%
A1ngel,_Nicol%C3%A1s_de_Vergara.jpg;
Author: Jl FilipC; License: Creative Commons Attribution-Share
Alike 4.0 International; Date: 9 April 2018; image modified
Pg. 65: Hannah prays for a child; From
www.commons.wikimedia.org; URL:
https://commons.wikimedia.org/wiki/File:Schnorr_von_Carolsfeld
_Bibel_in_Bildern_1860_086.png;
Author: Julis Schnorr von Carolsfeld; License: Public Domain;
Date: between 1851 and 1860; image modified
Pg. 66: The Visitation; From www.commons.wikimedia.org; URL:
https://commons.wikimedia.org/wiki/File:Visitation_MET_DP8833
57.jpg;
Author: Peeter van Lisebetten; License: Public Domain; Date:

circa 1656; License: Creative Commons CC0 1.0 Universal Public Domain Dedication; image modified

Pg. 67: Simeon holds the Christ Child; From www.commons.wikimedia.org; URL: https://commons.wikimedia.org/wiki/File:Loughrea_St._Brendan%27s_Cathedral_Baptistry_Window_Simeon_by_Michael_Healy_Detail_2019_09_05.jpg; Author: Andreas F. Borchert; License: Creative Commons Attribution-Share Alike 4.0 International; Date: 5 September 2019; image modified

Pg. 69: The Nativity; From www.commons.wikimedia.org; URL: https://commons.wikimedia.org/wiki/File:The_Bible_panorama,_or_The_Holy_Scriptures_in_picture_and_story_(1891)_(14598485757).jpg; Author: William A. Foster, The Bible Panorama; License: No Known Copyright Restrictions; Date 1891: image modified

Pg. 70: Body of the dead Christ; From www.commons.wikimedia.org; URL: https://commons.wikimedia.org/wiki/File:The_Entombment_MET_DP828161.jpg; Author: Paulus Pontius print made from a painting by Titian; License: Public Domain; Date: Between 1616 and 1657; image modified

Pg. 70: The Entombment; From www.commons.wikimedia.org; URL: https://commons.wikimedia.org/wiki/File:Snow_Storm-_March_5,_2015_(16733100552).jpg; Author: Johann Friedrich Overbeck; License: Creative Commons CC0 1.0 Universal Public Domain Dedication; Date: 1850; image modified

Pg. 71: The Crucifixion; From www.commons.wikimedia.org; URL: https://commons.wikimedia.org/wiki/File:Print_(BM_1891,0414.647_1).jpg; Author: print by Boetius Adamsz Bolswert after a work by Peter Paul Rubens; License: Public Domain; Date: 1631; image modified

Pg. 72: The feet of Christ washed and anointed; From www.commons.wikimedia.org; URL: https://commons.wikimedia.org/wiki/File:Print_(BM_R,3.65).jpg; Author: print by Michiel Natalis after Peter Paul Rubens; License: Public Domain; Date: between 1630 and 1668; image modified

Pg. 73: The washing of the feet of Christ; From www.commons.wikimedia.org; URL: https://commons.wikimedia.org/wiki/File:THY_SINS_ARE_FORGIVEN.jpg; Author: Heinrich Hofman; License: Public Domain; Date: 1893; image modified

Pg. 74: A man like lightning; From www.commons.wikimedia.org; URL: https://commons.wikimedia.org/wiki/File:Aegidius_Sadeler_II,_Joris_Hoefnagel,_Hans_von_Aachen_-_Salus_Generis_Humani_-_The_three_Maries_coming_to_the_Sepulchre_after_the_Resurrection.jpg; Author: Aegidius Sadeler after Hans von Aachen and

Joris Hoefnagel; License: Public Domain; Date: 1682-1699; Public Domain; image modified

Pg, 75: Mary Magdalen meets Jesus in the garden; From www.commons.wikimedia.org; URL: https://commons.wikimedia.org/wiki/File:Schnorr_von_Carolsfeld _Bibel_in_Bildern_1860_221.png; Author: Julis Schnorr von Carolsfeld; License: Public Domain; Date: between 1851 and 1860; image modified

Pg. 77: Mary Magdalen encounters Jesus in the garden; From www.commons.wikimedia.org; URL: https://commons.wikimedia.org/wiki/File:Christus_verschijnt_aan _Maria_Magdalena_en_de_Emma%C3%BCsgangers_Iesus_verschy nt_aan_Maria,_die_hem_voor_den_Hovenier_aanziet_Iesus_verv oegt_sich_by_twee_zyner_Discipelen_op_den_weg_van_Emma%C 3%BCs_(titel_op_object),_RP-P-1878-A-2376.jpg; Author: unknown; License: Creative Commons CC0 1.0 Universal Public Domain Dedication; Date: 1700; image modified

Pg. 78: Joseph ruling Egypt; From www.commons.wikimedia.org; URL: https://commons.wikimedia.org/wiki/File:The_Bible_and_its_story .._(1908)_(14760054041).jpg; Author: Charles F. Horne and Julius August Brewer; License: no known copyright restrictions; Date: 1908; image modified

Pg. 80: Jacob's Dream; From www.commons.wikimedia.org; URL: https://commons.wikimedia.org/wiki/File:The_Phillip_Medhurst_P icture_Torah_145._Jacob%27s_Dream._Genesis_cap_28_v_12._St othard.jpg; Author: Phillip Medhurst; LIcense: Creative Commons Attribution-Share Alike 3.0 Unreported; Date: 18 April 2014; image modified

Pg. 81: Jacob wrestles with an angel; From www.commons.wikimedia.org; URL: https://commons.wikimedia.org/wiki/File:The_Bible_panorama,_o r_The_Holy_Scriptures_in_picture_and_story_(1891)_(145981891 80).jpg; Author: William A. Foster in The Bible Panorama; License: no known copyright restrictions; Date: 1891; image modified

Pg. 82: The cloak of many colors, dipped in blood, is shown to Jacob; From www.commons.wikimedia.org; URL: https://commons.wikimedia.org/wiki/File:Joseph%27s_Bloody_Co at_is_Shown_to_Jacob_LACMA_44.2.6.jpg; Author: John Boydell; License: Public Domain; Date: 1782; image modified

Pg. 83: Joseph sold into slavery; From www.commons.wikimedia.org; URL: https://commons.wikimedia.org/wiki/File:Foster_Bible_Pictures_0 049-1_Jacob%27s_Sons_Selling_Their_Brother_Joseph.jpg; Author: Charles Foster; License: Public Domain; Date: 1897; image modified

Pg. 84: Joseph's dream; From www.commons.wikimedia.org; URL: https://commons.wikimedia.org/wiki/File:Holman_Josephs_Dream .jpg; Author: from the Holman Bible; License: Public Domain; Date: 1890; image modified

Pg. 85: Joseph's death in Egypt; From www.commons.wikimedia.org; URL: https://commons.wikimedia.org/wiki/File:Holman_Burying_the_B ody_of_Joseph.jpg; Author: from the Holman Bible; License: Public Domain; Date: 1890; image modified

Pg. 86: The Panagia Tricherousam, "The All-Holy with Three Hands"; From www.commons.wikimedia.org; URL: https://commons.wikimedia.org/wiki/File:VergineTricherusa.jpg; Author: unknown; License: Public Domain; Date: unknown; image modified

Pg. 89: Bas relief in wood of Our Lady healing the hand of St. John of Damascus; From www.commons.wikimedia.org; URL: https://commons.wikimedia.org/wiki/File:Wei%C3%9Fenau_Chorg est%C3%BChl_links_Dorsalfeld_11_Johannes_von_Damaskus.jpg; Authors: Andreas Priefcke; License: Creative Commons Attribution 3.0 Unreported; Date: April 2011; image modified

Pg. 93: St. Andrew's Church with statue of St. Cuthman; From www.commons.wikimedia.org; URL: https://commons.wikimedia.org/w/index.php?search=Steyning%2 C_The_Church_of_St_Andrew_and_St_Cuthman_-_geograph.org.uk_-_4333565&title=Special:MediaSearch&go=Go&type=image; Author: Michael Garlick; License: Creative Commons Attribution-Share Alike 2.0 Generic; Date: 2 February 2015; image modified

Pg. 96: St. Andrew's Church with statue of St. Cuthman; From www.commons.wikimedia.org; URL: https://commons.wikimedia.org/wiki/File:Sculpture_of_St._Cuthm an_on_St._Cuthman%27s_Field_opposite_the_church_-_geograph.org.uk_-_970277.jpg; Author: Pam Fray; License: Creative Commons Attribution-Share Alike 2.0 Generic; Date: 18 September 2008; image modified

Pg. 97: baby clothes; image by Jake Frost

Pg. 98: Compass Point Storm Tower; From www.commons.wikimedia.org; URL: https://commons.wikimedia.org/wiki/File:Compass_Point,_Bude.j pg; Author: Nilfanion; License: Creative Commons Attribution-Share Alike 3.0 Unreported; Date: 8 June 2011; image modified

Pg. 99: Compass Point storm tower; From www.commons.wikimedia.org; URL: https://commons.wikimedia.org/wiki/File:Tower_on_Compass_Poi nt_-_geograph.org.uk_-_1548880.jpg; Author: Phillip Halling; License: Creative Commons Attribution-Share Alike 2.0 Generic;

Date: 28 September 2009; image modified

Pg. 100: Winston Churchill at Whitehall on VE Day, May 8, 1945; From www.commons.wikimedia.org; URL: https://commons.wikimedia.org/wiki/File:Winston_Churchill_wav es_to_crowds_in_Whitehall_in_London_as_they_celebrate_VE_Da y,_8_May_1945._H41849.jpg; Authors: War Office official photographer Major W. G. Horton; License: Public Domain; Date: 8 May 1945; image modified

Pg. 101: Winston Churchill flying to Bermuda; From www.commons.wikimedia.org; URL: https://commons.wikimedia.org/wiki/File:1942-01-16_WinstonChurchill_Boeing314_CaptainsSeat.jpg; Author: Captain Horton; License: Public Domain; Date: 16 January 1942; image modified

Pg. 102: Sower; From www.commons.wikimedia.org; URL: https://commons.wikimedia.org/wiki/File:The_sower_(Boston_Pu blic_Library).jpg; Author: Winslow Homer; License: Public Domain; Date: circa 1880; image modified

Pg. 103: God creating; From www.commons.wikimedia.org; URL: https://commons.wikimedia.org/wiki/File:God_Creating_the_Sun, _the_Moon,_and_the_Stars_LACMA_65.37.55.jpg; Author: Antonio Tempesta; License: Public Domain; Date: circa 1600; image modified

Pg. 105: Airplane wing; From www.commons.wikimedia.org; URL: https://commons.wikimedia.org/wiki/File:A_wing_tip_of_an_airpl ane_(40118125441).jpg; Authors: U.S. Department of Agriculture; License: Public Domain; Date: 6 February 2018; image modified

Pg. 106: John Winthrop; From www.commons.wikimedia.org; URL: https://commons.wikimedia.org/wiki/File:John_Winthrop_by_Rich ard_Saltonstall_Greenough_(1873).jpg; Author: statue by Richard Saltonstall Greenough, photograph by Daderot; License: Public Domain; Date: statue created in 1873, photograph taken 19 September 2005; image modified

Pg. 109: woodcut of ship; From www.commons.wikimedia.org; URL: https://commons.wikimedia.org/wiki/File:Reddragonship.jpg; Author: unknown author; License: Public Domain; Date: cica 1600's; image modified

Pg. 110: Cornucopia of Harvest; From www.commons.wikimedia.org; URL: https://commons.wikimedia.org/wiki/File:Page_180.jpg; Author: uploaded by Sue Clark; License: Public Domain; Date: uploaded 6 August 2009; image modified

Pg. 112: ghosts in trees; image by Jake Frost

Pg. 113: Jack O 'Lanterns; image by Jake Frost

Pg. 114: owl; From www.commons.wikimedia.org; URL:

https://commons.wikimedia.org/wiki/File:Owl_Drawing_(1).jpg;
Author: unknown; License: Public Domain; Date: 1853; image
modified

Pg. 114: fox; From www.commons.wikimedia.org; URL:
https://commons.wikimedia.org/wiki/File:Die_Gartenlaube_(1858)
_b_333.jpg; Author: Guido Hammer; License: Public Domain;
Date: 1858; image modified

Pg. 115; mouse; From www.commons.wikimedia.org; URL:
https://commons.wikimedia.org/wiki/File:Americana_1920_Mous
e_-_Mice.jpg; Author: unknown; License: Public Domain; Date:
1920; image modified

Pg. 116; fresh snow; From www.commons.wikimedia.org; URL:
https://commons.wikimedia.org/wiki/File:Fresh_snow,_Blacktail_
Deer_Plateau_(43965900031).jpg; Author: Yellowstone National
Park, Neal Herbert; License: Public Domain; Date: 19 February
2018; image modified

Pg. 117: Crescent Moon; From www.commons.wikimedia.org;
URL:
https://commons.wikimedia.org/wiki/File:Crescent_Moon_(62051
15071).jpg; Authors: grace_kat; License: Creative Commons
Attribution-Share Alike 2.0 Generic; Date: 30 September 2011;
image modified

Pg. 118: wolf; From www.commons.wikimedia.org; URL:
https://commons.wikimedia.org/wiki/File:Picture_Natural_History
_-_No_4_-_The_Wolf.png; Author: Mary E. C. Boutell; License:
Public Domain; Date: 1869; image modified

Pg. 120: Snow; From www.commons.wikimedia.org; URL:
https://commons.wikimedia.org/wiki/File:Kafka_W_krainach_wiec
znego_lodu_Rys._9.jpg; Author: unknown; License: Public Domain;
Date: 1907; image modified

Pg. 121: church bell tower in the snow; From
www.commons.wikimedia.org; URL:
https://commons.wikimedia.org/wiki/File:A_Christmas_Carol_-
_006.png; Author: John A. Hows; License: Public Domain; Date:
1864; image modified

Pg. 122: The Nativity; From www.commons.wikimedia.org; URL:
https://commons.wikimedia.org/wiki/File:Compass_Point,_Bude.j
pg; Author: Jan Harmensz Muller; License: Creative Commons CCO
1.0 Universal Public Domain Dedication; Date: circa 1626; image
modified

Pg. 127: Balaam sees The Star; From
www.commons.wikimedia.org; URL:
https://commons.wikimedia.org/wiki/File:The_Bible_and_its_story
.._(1908)_(14586389969).jpg; Author: Charles F. Horne, Julius
August Brewar; License: no known copyright restrictions; Date:
1908; image modified

Pg. 129: Angels come to the shepherds in the fields; From www.commons.wikimedia.org; URL: https://commons.wikimedia.org/wiki/File:The_angels_tells_the_sh epherd_that_Jesus_is_born.jpg; Authors: unknown; License: Public Domain; Date: 1873; image modified

Pg. 130: Our Lady holding Jesus; From www.commons.wikimedia.org; URL: https://commons.wikimedia.org/wiki/File:St._Henry_Church_-_Madonna_and_Jesus.jpg; Author: Nheyob; License: Creative Commons Attribution-Share Alike 3.0 Unreported; Date: 12 March 2011; image modified

Pg. 132: The Three Wise Men following The Star; From www.commons.wikimedia.org; URL: https://commons.wikimedia.org/wiki/File:The_Bible_panorama,_o r_The_Holy_Scriptures_in_picture_and_story_(1891)_(145982957 40).jpg; Author: William A. Foster; License: No Known Copy Right Restrictions; Date: circa 1891; image modified

Pg. 133: Adoration of the Magi; From www.commons.wikimedia.org; URL: https://commons.wikimedia.org/wiki/File:THE_ADORATION_OF_T HE_MAGI.jpg; Author: Heinrich Hofmann; License: Public Domain; Date: 1893; image modified

Pg. 137: Adoration of the Shepherds; From www.commons.wikimedia.org; URL: https://commons.wikimedia.org/wiki/File:Aanbidding_door_de_he rders,_RP-P-OB-7136.jpg; Authors: Federico Zuccaro and Cornelius Cort, held in collection of the Rijksmuseum; License: Creative Commons OOC 1.0 Universal Public Domain Dedication; Date: circa 1565; image modified

Pg. 151: Adoration of the Shepherds; From www.commons.wikimedia.org; URL: https://commons.wikimedia.org/wiki/File:Aanbidding_door_de_he rders,_RP-P-OB-7136.jpg; Author: Donatus Dabravolskas; Date: 31 January 2019; License: Creative Commons Attribution-Share Alike 4.0 International; image modified

About the Author

Jake Frost is the author of seven previous books:

(1) *The Light of Caliburn*, an Arthurian fantasy adventure novel set in modern times which won an Honorable Mention from the Catholic Media Association;

(2) *Catholic Dad, (Mostly) Funny Stories of Faith, Family and Fatherhood*;

(3) *Catholic Dad 2, More (Mostly) Funny Stories of Faith, Family, and Fatherhood*;

(4) *The Happy Jar*, a children's picture book that Frost also illustrated;

(5) *From Dust to Stars, Poems by Jake Frost*;

(6) *Victory! Poems by Jake Frost*; and

(7) *Wings Upon the Unseen Gust, Poems by Jake Frost*, which also won an Honorable Mention from the Catholic Media Association.

He is a husband, father of five, and a lawyer, living in a small town in the American Midwest.

Made in the USA
Monee, IL
01 April 2024

56149090R00085